MONEY MYTHS

THE MILLIONAIRE MINDSET

BY
MAX MAXWELL

TABLE OF CONTENTS

WAKING UP
TO YOUR
GREATNESS

Money Myths: A Millionaire Mindset 3

What would you say if I told you that having more money isn't so much about changing the way you work as much as it is changing the way you think? And what if I told you that you have the ability to make as much money as you want? It's what I refer to as the abundance mindset.

Would you say I was crazy?
Cappin? Not making any sense?

I certainly understand that. After all, for our entire lives, we've been told that the only way to have more money is to either:

- Win the lottery
- Work harder

The odds of you winning the lottery are small – and besides, there's a much smarter way to make money.

And while there's certainly some truth that you must work hard if you want money, you can have as much money as

Does this describe you?

Moving Forward Mentally
Focused on your goals
Tuning out that "Noise"

If so, you are one of the few, many are :

- Not reaching their true potential.
- Not financially free.
- Not truly happy.
- Asleep at the wheel.

If You know that you should be achieving great things...

...but you just can't quite seem to get there.

Then this book is for you.

This book will teach you how to change your mindset and truly change your life. It will blow up many of the myths that you've believed for years and reshape your thinking as a whole.

The only prerequisite for reading this book is an open mind.

Some of what you're about to read may contradict beliefs you've held about yourself and money for years. These beliefs have been holding you back from reaching your true potential.

It's time for those beliefs to be put to rest and for you to embrace the true reality of who you are.

It's time to stop being unconscious – comfortable in the matrix that is life – and put action behind your words.

Ready?

Let's get started.

COMMON MYTHS REGARDING MONEY

There's a good chance that what you believe about money is simply wrong. We've been conditioned by society, by our parents, and by our friends to believe certain things about money.

And most of us have believed those things without EVER questioning them.

When I was living with My Mom at 30, I had the same thoughts about money that many of you reading this book currently have. Making a Million dollars was a pipe-dteam... Hell I'd even be happy with 6-Figures at that point... But even then I was limiting myself to the true potential and the true amount of money that I can make. Removing this mental limit, is the first step to making more, and being financially free.

As a result of societal conditioning, we have what you might call a complicated relationship with money.

- *We want more of it* but can't ever seem to get enough.

- *If I had a lot of money everyone* would change how they look at me.

- *We're grateful when we have the money to purchase the things we want*, but also feel like we're being selfish in some cases compared to others.

Why do we have this relationship with money?

It's because of the myths and lies about money.

And we've never questioned our beliefs to see if they're actually true. And because we've never questioned them, we haven't achieved the level of success that we truly want.

When I was 30, with negative dollars in my bank account, I assumed I would end up stuck at my Moms house forever. Because I never questioned the belief that I was the reason for my lack of success. When in reality, I was on the breaking point of a mindset that had been holding me back for so many years... I pushed back and questioned my beliefs, beliefs about society, beliefs about myself, and I taught myself how to wholesale real-estate. Which in turn made me the first millionaire in my family. A feat I absolutely would never have seen me accomplishing.

If you want more success, money, and happiness, then it's crucial that you stop believing money myths and master your mindset about money.

Mastering your money mindset requires dispelling the myths you've believed for so long.

Let's look at some of the common myths we've believed about money.

MONEY MYTH #1: MONEY IS EVIL

We've all heard it said that money is the root of all evil. Maybe your parents reinforced this myth when you were growing up. Maybe they told you to stay humble or always save your money and find a good paying job as bills and life come at you fast.

And so, you've unconsciously adopted this belief.

- You don't want to accumulate too much money because you're afraid that it will change you.

- You believe that somehow money will turn you morally wrong or egotistic.

MYTH #2 PEOPLE WHO HAVE MONEY DON'T CARE ABOUT OTHERS

Many of us carry around the assumption that only people who are greedy want more money. We assume that if we want money, we'll become like Ebenezer Scrooge, always hoarding money but never giving it away.

But is this true?

No.

Again having a lot of money isn't bad. It's what you do with the money that truly matters

Yes, some people are greedy and simply want to accumulate as much money as possible.

But, generally having more money also allows you to Be Extremely generous.
 It allows you to give things to others in need, donate to charity's the list goes on.

You simply can't do those things if you don't have money.

You have to be selfish, to be self-less.

You can't be generous if you don't have money.

Think about that for a minute.

If you want to be financially generous, you have to have some finances in the first place.

It's time to kill this myth. Wanting more money does not make you greedy.

MYTH #3: MONEY DOESN'T GROW ON TREES!

If you grew up in a house where finances were regularly "tight", then you may harbor the belief that there is not enough money.

You believe that the reason you don't have enough money is because there isn't enough money to go around.

But let's step back a minute and evaluate this belief.

How much money is in the world?

Trillions and trillions of dollars, and they print more and more every day.

There is more than enough money for everyone. We could currently give every person in the world a million dollars right now, that's a lot of money.

As you can see there is an actual *abundance* of money in the world.

Just because you don't have all the money in the world doesn't mean that there's not enough money to go around.

This is the difference between a "scarcity" mindset and an "abundance" mindset:

- *With a scarcity mindset, you believe that there is never enough.* You feel like you have to hold onto everything you have because you never know when it will be gone.

- *With an abundance mindset, you believe that there is more than enough for everyone.* When you get money, it doesn't mean that someone else is not getting money.

So, as you see, *money is not a zero-sum game.* In other words, you earning money does *not* mean that someone else is losing money.

That's not how it works.

There is more than enough money in the world for everyone to have as much as they want.

Let's kill this myth. There's plenty for everyone. Choose to live in a world of abundance.

MYTH #4: I'LL NEVER MAKE ENOUGH MONEY

If you believe that you'll never make enough money, then you certainly will never make enough money.

But why do you have that belief in the first place?

If there is more than enough money in the world for everyone, why should you believe that you'll never make enough?

You're an incredibly talented person that has so much to offer the world, and it's critical that you believe it. Your skills, talents, and expertise are valuable, and there are lots of people out there who are willing to pay for those skills.

But in order for this to be your reality, you must believe it first.

You have to stop buying into the negative self talk. That you'll never make enough money and start telling yourself that you are going to make more than you could imagine.

You may not know exactly how you're going to make the money, but that's okay.

Master your mindset, and the money will soon follow.

Let's kick this myth to the curb. You can and will make more than enough money if you're willing to believe it first.

MYTH #5: IF I MAKE MORE MONEY, PEOPLE WON'T LIKE ME

This is a common myth that many people believe, especially if their parents didn't like people who had money.

But the reality is we don't dislike people who make money. We dislike people who flaunt their wealth in an arrogant way.

Again, this goes back to how you use your money.

If you make more money and then start bragging to your friends about how awesome you are, then sure, they might not like you anymore.

But if you use your increased income to help others, people will actually like you more! And they certainly won't begrudge you for spending some on yourself.

This myth needs to go far away.

You can't bring everyone with you to the top. No one elses opinion matters in your life except your own.

MYTH #6: I'M JUST FINE WITHOUT MONEY

If you've struggled for a long time to achieve financial stability, then you may have convinced yourself that you're just fine without having any money.

But is this really true?

- Are you really living your absolute best life?
- Are you the best version of yourself that you can be?
- Are you able to live fearlessly, generously, and joyfully?

Let's be honest: money makes many things possible that aren't possible otherwise.

Money allows you to travel the world, Deepen Friendships and Support Worthy Causes.

If you don't have money, you don't have the fhe freedom to be your best self. Money gives you options and time... money without time and time without money are equally difficult situations to be in.

Let's be done with this myth. *It's time for you to achieve your true greatness.*

THE POWER OF YOUR MIND: HAVING AN ABUNDANCE MINDSET

Your mind is an incredibly powerful thing. Far more powerful than you can even imagine.

What you think about has an incredible effect on the quality of your life and whether you reach your dreams. In fact, your brain controls most of your reality:

- What you think about...
- What you give your attention to...
- What you focus on...

...literally controls the outcomes in your life.

My good friend Coach Lynch Hunt said on my podcast:

"Today is a gift, that's why they call it the present, you may be holding onto a subconscious belief that is hurting you. You can stand by and reinforce old beliefs all your life, or you can learn from my life and let go of the beliefs which do not make your life better"

This is true. The joy of your life and the reality you create depends primarily upon your thoughts. That's how powerful your brain is.

If you want to attract wealth,
it's crucial to adopt an abundance mindset.

You must have a mindset of abundance.

Because of this, it's essential
that we learn to master the way we think
about wealth.

YOUR MIND CONTROLS YOUR OUTCOMES

What most people fail to realize is that their mind creates almost all of the outcomes in their lives. Every outcome you're experiencing right now, whether it's positive or negative, is primarily the result of your thoughts.

Or, to put it another way, what you constantly think about shapes your reality.

Your focus determines what you attract:

- Focus on positive things and you'll attract positive things.
- Focus on negative things and you'll attract the negative.

Yes, your mind really is that powerful. Again, as Coach Lynch said:

> *you may be holding onto a subconscious belief that is hurting you. You can stand by and reinforce old beliefs all your life, or you can learn from life and let go of the beliefs which do not make your life better"*

And one of my favorites from Coach:

> *Thoughts become actions; actions become habits; and habits eventually become beliefs. Destructive beliefs will hurt you and everyone around you. Positive beliefs will lift you up and others through you.*

Are you starting to get the picture? As Coach said, your outer world (reality) is simply a reflection of your inner world (your thoughts, desires, and dreams).

If you're not experiencing what you want in your life, it's primarily due to what's happening in your inner world.

- Not attracting the wealth you want? Inner mindset.
- Not able to get your head above water financially? Inner mindset.
- Not able to move forward in your job like you should? Inner Mindset.

The good news is that you are the one in control of your mindset.

You determine what you think about and focus on. The more you control and shape your inner world, the more you will control and shape your actual reality.

Isn't that amazing to think about?

The massive implication is that if you want to change your life and attract more wealth, you absolutely must master the way you think.

CHANGING YOUR MIND ABOUT MONEY

If your outer world is a reflection of your inner world, then it's absolutely essential that you master your abundance mindset

You need to be done with the myths from your past and adopt an abundance mindset.

If you have a scarcity mindset, believing that there is never enough money, then that is exactly what you will attract into your life. You will attract scarcity. You attract exactly what you focus on.

But if you believe in the abundance of the world, you'll attract abundance into your life. If you believe that there is more than enough for you and everyone else, you'll begin manifesting that in your life.

What you believe becomes your reality.

Therefore, it's important to believe:

- There's enough money for everyone.
- You simply need to reach out and take it.

Think about all the abundance in the world. You simply need to open yourself up to receive it.

Whether you believe in God or universal intelligence or the energy behind all things, you must believe that it wants you to have money. Because it really does.

The world is full of abundance, and if you're living in scarcity, then you're not enjoying all that the world has to offer.

It's time to change your mindset about money. To believe that there's enough, that *you* deserve to have money, and that you were created to experience abundance.

Regularly affirm this. I personally do daily affirmations every morning. Tell yourself these things over and over again until they're burned into your brain. Until you believe them with all your heart and soul.

OPPORTUNITIES ARE EVERYWHERE STOP DELETING THEM.

Once you start having an abundance mindset and open yourself up to all that the world wants to give you, you'll start seeing opportunities everywhere.

- You'll see ways to acquire money that you never would have seen before.

- Opportunities will drop into your lap out of nowhere.

- You'll begin to attract money in ways that surprise you.

But you must open your mind to the possibilities that are all around you. The world is full of infinite possibilities, and just because you can't see them doesn't mean they're not there.

At WELIVE 2019, I talked about opportunity:

> You can't see your opportunities, because you delete them. You must know what you want before you get it, and for that to happen you have to know what you want and don't want.
>
> I've asked people what they want in life, and often they start telling you things that they don't want. This is because their mind is focused on the negative stuff verses the positive. The mind distorts everything that you see and experience. When successful people see things, they look at it as it is, and then they try to create an opportunity out of it. A cup half-full vs. a cup half-empty

Today, choose the path of positivity and abundance.

One of the best ways to choose abundance is through the practice of gratitude.

Start practicing gratitude for all the ways that the Universe has got your back and is bringing abundance into your life. When you receive something good and positive, say a simple, "Thank you." This practice will start to transform the way you live.

When you're grateful for even the smallest things, it puts positive energy out into the world, which then attracts more positive things into your life.

It really is a powerful cycle. You put out the positive energy of gratitude and you are rewarded with more things to be grateful for.

So, begin practicing gratitude immediately. As you shift your mindset from scarcity to abundance, you'll be shocked by all the good things that start to come into your life.

TAKING ACTION
ON YOUR DREAMS

Abundance mindset is absolutely necessary if you want to attract wealth and build your dreams.

But an abundance mindset alone is not enough.

ACTION is needed.

You must start taking action on your dreams.

When you have an abundance mindset *and* you start taking action on your dreams...

...you truly become limitless.

There is absolutely nothing that can stop you. You will achieve more than you thought possible.

In other words, you may have an abundance mindset, but if you don't start taking action on your dreams, nothing will change.

Abundance mindset combined with action leads to great things.

The equation is:

Mindset + Action = Dreams Become Reality

Once you start taking action, you'll begin to see the things you dreamed about becoming a reality.

When taking action on your dreams, follow these steps...

STEP #1: WRITE DOWN YOUR DREAMS

The first step is to write down your dreams and goals. Be as specific as possible when writing them down. So you can see them in your mind's eye.

Ask yourself questions like:

- What do I want to get out of life?
- What are my TRUE GOALS?
- What do I want to be known for?
- How much money do I want to make?
- Can I change my Family Tree?

The more concrete you can be when writing down your dreams and goals, the more you'll be able to visualize them coming true.

The more you can visualize them, the more positive emotion you'll feel around them and the more focused you'll be on them.

And the more focused you are on your dreams, the more you'll attract them into your life.

It's really that simple.

Thoughts lead to feelings. Feelings lead to actions. Actions lead to results.

So, write down your dreams and goals with as many details as possible. Feel them intensely. Feel how amazing it will be when you accomplish them.

These feelings will lead to actions, which will then translate into amazing results.

After you've written down your dreams, rehearse them again and again. Repeat them to yourself every single day. Affirm that they are going to come true.

Say things like:

- "I am going to double my income by XX date."
- "I am a financial success in all areas of my life."
- "I will break the company sales record this year"
- This will be my best year ever financially."

Repeat these affirmations again and again until you engrain the positivity into your mind.

Raise your energy level and feelings around these affirmations until you're ready to take big actions on them.

Even if you don't know how these things are going to happen, affirm that they will. These kinds of affirmations create positive energy around you that will keep you motivated and on track.

"Everyone Underestimates the power of hard work and Visualization."

If you put out positive energy in the form of affirmations and gratitude, you'll see that positive energy coming back to you in positive forms.

STEP #2: START TAKING ACTION ON YOUR DREAMS

Once you've written down your dreams and begun to rehearse them each day, it's crucial to start taking action.

Map out what specific steps you need to follow in order to achieve your dreams, and then begin taking those actions.

What do you need to do in order to make your dreams a reality? Don't worry if you don't have this all figured out.

Start by mapping out where you can take action.

- Do you need to call someone?
- Hire a mentor?
- Start building another business on the side?

- Send an email to an important contact?
- Call a friend you haven't spoken to in a while?

If you have an abundance mindset and are open to new opportunities, You'll start to notice problems that need solutions. In business, a solution, is your product.

Take action on these ideas. These are cues that are intended to guide you on the path to wealth and success.

Make it your goal to take action on your goals every single day. Consistency is key, try to move at least a little bit closer to that goal. If you don't focus at some point daily, you aren't going to win.

When something comes to your mind, take action on it.

The more you take action, the more you'll realize that you truly do have limitless potential. You'll achieve things you never believed were possible.

YOUR DREAMS ARE WAITING FOR YOU

And now for the million-dollar question:

What are your kids and grandkids going to remember you for? What is society going to remember you for?

You now know that:

- You truly have limitless potential.
- Most of the myths you've believed about money are totally false.
- Your mindset controls your reality.
- You have the power to shape your reality.
- You can attract and manifest the wealth and dreams that you desire.

Are you going to start taking action on your dreams? Or are you going to continue living asleep at the wheel, walking through life mostly unconscious?

Are you going to take control of your destiny, master your money mindset, and achieve your dreams, or are you going to continue struggling?

There is an amazing future out there, just waiting for you to seize it. Don't let that future pass you by. Don't arrive 30 years from now and regret the actions that you didn't take.

Master your abundance mindset today and watch what begins to happen. You'll notice more and more opportunities for success, just be open minded and never be afraid to learn a new skill.

I've seen hundreds if not thousands find outlets that let them get closer to reaching their goal, all it took was realizing that you are your biggest obstacle between you and your dreams.

Your mindset is everything, master it.

ENJOYED THE BOOK?

LEAVE A REVIEW!

ALSO BE SURE TO CHECK OUT OUR PDF DOWNLOAD WHERE YOU CAN REFLECT ON YOUR OWN MINDSET BELOW

HTTPS://MMLINK.IO/AFFIRMATIONS

Made in the USA
Monee, IL
01 April 2021

63414660R00031